Diabetes Never Again

Frederick Mickel Huck

authorHOUSE®

AuthorHouse™
1663 Liberty Drive
Bloomington, IN 47403
www.authorhouse.com
Phone: 1-800-839-8640

First published by AuthorHouse   8/25/2011

ISBN: 978-1-4567-5914-8 (sc)
ISBN: 978-1-4567-5915-5 (e)

Library of Congress Control Number: 2011907934

Printed in the United States of America

This book is dedicated to:

ROBERT E MENZIE

INEZ A MENZIE

DONALD W HUCK

AURA V HUCK

DR EDE KOENIG

Special thanks to:

SANDRA V MOONEY

MATTHEW F MOONEY

JOHN DUNLAP

ANGIE INGERSOLL

Facts Of Diabetes

Diabetes is a disease that is caused by consuming the wrong type of foods that do not have the proper nutrition that the human body requires. Most of the people who are diagnosed with diabetes have family members who are also suffering the disease because their food choices are similar. Babies that are born with the disease have been inflicted with it because their mothers have made bad choices in their food selection during pregnancy. Diabetes did not use to be a major problem in the western world because "junk food" (food without nutrition) was not produced. Only since the advent of fast foods has diabetes become a problem.

Unfortunately, drugs cannot cure or prevent diabetes, the most that drugs can do is maintain the affliction. Pharmaceuticals are making billions of dollars a year by maintaining the disease, but are not curing it, and the percentage of people becoming diabetic increases. Obviously drugs are not the cure for diabetes and causing more harm than good. Diabetes does not need to be permanent, it is foreign to the human body and is not natural.

Diabetes is a slow killer, but never the less it can be a deadly killer. It lowers the quality of ones life and often leads to amputations, blindness, and other unpleasant problems before it kills. The best way to diagnose diabetes is to check ones sugar level in your urine; it is one hundred percent accurate, if done in four consecutive readings using a hand refractometer. A blood check can also be used, but it is not very accurate. Diabetes is at epidemic levels and is effecting people of all ages from the very young to the very old. However, diabetes is very easy to prevent and it is reversible and does not have to be permanent, unless Drugs are used and then the disease will be permanent. The right food choices is the only way to avoid this horrible disease.

Myths of Diabetes

- Diabetes is caused and based on genes-- heredity.

- Drugs control diabetes.

- In the US diabetes is only on the rise due to easier access to medical attention.

- In poor counties diabetes is much lower due to the lack of medical diagnois.

- If there is a history of diabetes in your family, you will also be a diabetic.

- The medical establishment wants to cure diabetes.

- Only a doctor can treat diabetes.

- The side effects of the drugs are a fair trade verus the symptoms of diabetes.

- Doctors do not know the cause of diabetes.

Facts of Diabetes

- Diabetes is caused by the lack of real food packed with nutrition.

- Family members who have diabetes are eating similar junk foods.

- Babies who are born with diabetes, the mother is eating junk food.

- Historically there was very little diabetes in the United States.

- Drugs do not have any thing to do with the prevention of diabetes.

- Doctors are not informing patients of all the side effects of the assigned drugs.

- All drugs will harm the body and cause more problems.

- The medical doctors will maintain your diabetes with their advice given.

- The medical system makes billions on diabetes yearly.

- Herbal Golden Seal is a natural insulin (this is theraputic).

- Diabetes is on the rise in the United States and is the highest in the world.

- Diabetes is foreign to the human body.

- Diabetes is not premanent.

- Diabetes is not natural.

- With very few exceptions most people are not aware of the lowered quality of life caused by living with diabetes.

- Checking sugar in the blood is not accurate.

- Checking sugar in the urine is 100% accurate and requires four consecutive readings before any action is taken, (Hand Refractometer is needed).

- There are more young people with diabetes than ever before. This is at epidemic levels.

- The lack of drugs are not the cause of diabetes.

- Diabetes does not just happen on its own.

- Most people are not aware how easy diabetes can be prevented.

- Diabetes is reversable and not permanent. I used to have diabetes. Its very easy to get rid of diabetes. I find diabetes is so much harder to maintain. Diabetes never again

Conclusion

It is not alarming to me to read the latest statistics of the rising rates of diabetes. With the same old tired methods being used by the doctors to treat diabetes, it really is not of any suprise by definition why epidemic levels of diabetes exists at this magnatude.

In the last fifty years the large medical system offers more doctors, more drugs, more research, and yet there is even more diabetes? I said more every year! This is what everyone with diabetes should be asking, but do not stop there, move on, take charge of your body! It is so easy! The information in this book will be a good guide of how I was able to eleminate diabetes and have no desire to have diabetes return.

I will say it again, if I had continued to listen to doctors advice, today I will still have diabetes. Instead I cleaned out my colon, put only real food in my body, and cut down my exercise approximately 90%, and diabetes was eliminated! Nowdays I do not have any desire to bring diabetes back into my life—diabetes never again!

Fourteen Days Guide

The purpose of this fourteen-day meal plan is to illustrate that starvation does not exist when following the plan. Instead of listing the fruit on a daily log everyday, I just list here approximately, what was eaten. For the last two years, I have reversed my two meals. The larger was consumed first and the second is mostly raw. Prior to eating breakfast, generally a half an hour after I wake, I drink a quart of warm water with two teaspoons of lemon juice, one tablespoon of inland sea water, and one tablespoon of silver mineral water. I consume approximately five pounds of fruit daily, and the fruit varies according to the seasons of the year. The fourteen days are very similar (fruit meal) and they are three different colors of apples, twelve cherries, one nectarine, one mango, one slice of pineapple, one slice of cantaloupe, eight green grapes, one apricot, and one peach,. In addition I also eat eight raw Brazil nuts, six apricot nuts, one teaspoon of sunflower seeds, one teaspoon of pumpkin seeds, two capsules of calcium, two capsules of magnesium. For dinner, I usually have a salad, which consists of red or green head lettuce three radishes cut small one long green, onion cut small one third of a carrot, cut small one half of avocado one half of celery stalk, cut small six tablespoons of lemon juice approximately one tablespoon or more of Braggs Ammino up to twelve ounces or more of two different kinds of Hot Sauce bread, or crackers, or corn tortillas.

Please do not copy or give away any material, not just, because it is copyright protected material, but doing this will interfere with my program of feeding and educating the unhealthy. All book proceeds as of 2008 have gone into this program. Instead my wish is that you do share your cooking with friends, family, and strangers.

Questions, concerns, and suggestions are welcome:

7619 N "8th" St
Fresno, CA 93720-2644
Phone 559 435 4069

14 Days of Meals

Day 1

Breakfast: Raw Nut Mix Combination

Fresh fruit

Herb and Garlic Baked Rice

Dinner: Salad

Garlic Bread

Tostados

Havanero Rice

Dessert: Cinnamon Ice Cream

Notes: _____

_____

_____

Day 2

Breakfast: Raw nut mix combination

Fresh fruit

Popcorn

Dinner: Salad

Corn tortillas

Tomato casserole

Dessert: Cherry cream pie

Notes: _____

_____

_____

Day 3

Breakfast: Raw nut mix combination

Fresh fruit

Cashew waffles

Dinner: Salad

Lavish Tonir bread

Tamale bean pie

Dessert: Hazel nut fudge

Notes: _____

_____

_____

Day 4

Breakfast: Raw nut mix combination

Fresh fruit

Toast and Cherry jam

Dinner: Salad

Crackers

Roast

Dessert: Peach Cream pie

Notes: _____

_____

_____

Day 5

Breakfast: Raw nut mix combination

Fresh fruit

Cajon dry roasted nut mix

Dinner: Salad

Corn bread

Pocket pizzas

Dessert: Carob roasted nut mix

Notes: _____

_____

_____

Day 6

Breakfast: Raw nut mix combination

Fresh fruit

Toast with Plum jam

Dinner: Salad

Corn tortillas

Stuffed Bell peppers

Dessert: Peach cup cookies

Notes: _____
_____
_____

Day 7

Breakfast: Raw nut mix combination

Fresh fruit

Havanero rice

Dinner: Salad

Crackers

Spanish pasta

Dessert: Plum cup cookies

Notes: _____

_____

_____

Day 8

Breakfast: Raw nut mix combination

               Fresh fruit

               Pumpkin seed waffles

Dinner: Salad

               Lavish-tonir

               Bread

               Cajon rice

               Double baked potatoes

Dessert: Maple syrup cookies

Notes: _____

               _____

               _____

Day 9

Breakfast: Raw nut mix combination

Fresh fruit

Walnut waffles

Dinner: Salad

Corn bread

Potato and cabbage soup

Dessert: Cinnamon Tofu cookies

Notes: _____

_____

_____

Day 10

Breakfast: Raw nut mix combination

               Fresh fruit

               Bell pepper rice

Dinner: Salad

               Crackers

               Egg rolls

               Chinese rice

Dessert: Pecan rope cookies

Notes: _____

               _____

               _____

Day 11

Breakfast: Raw nut mix combination

Fresh fruit

Pancakes

Dinner: Salad

Lavish tonir bread

Enchiladas

Spanish rice

Dessert: Licorice Ice cream

Notes: _____

_____

_____

Day 12

Breakfast: Raw nut mix combination

Fresh fruit,

Black-eyed pea rice

Dinner: Salad

Garlic toast

Pot pie

Dessert: Carob macaroons

Notes: _____

_____

_____

Day 13

Breakfast: Raw nut mix combination

Fresh fruit

Oatmeal

Dinner: Lavish tonir bread

Taco salad

Green pepper rice

Dessert: English toffee candy

Notes: _____

_____

_____

Day 14

Breakfast: Raw nut mix combination

Fresh fruit

Toast with Apricot jam

Dinner: Salad

Lavish tonir bread

Bean Burritos

Jamaican rice

Dessert: Licorice Caramels

Notes: _____

_____

_____

Recipe 342————————————————————

HAZEL NUT CARMEL CANDY

Place the following into a vitamix for 5 minutes.

   One half cup of soymilk
   2 teaspoons of vanilla
   One half cup of sucanant sugar
   1 cup of maple syrup
   1 teaspoon of Biosalt
   One large apple or two small (remove core only)

Then pour into a medium size pan. In addition, boil on warm for 50 - 60 minutes, stir occasionally and prepare dish below:

Line a glass dish 8 X 8 inch with parchment paper and add:

One cup of Hazelnuts (chopped) inside dish and set aside.

Start freezer test 45 minutes into boiling.

Freezer test:

Place in a small dish one spoon of the above mixture and place dish in freezer for one minute.

Mixture should be harder at 50 minutes into boiling, repeat freezer test at 55 minutes, mixture will be even harder.

At 60 minutes, mixture should be complete. Pour mixture into glass dish 8 X 8 inch and place in refrigerator uncovered, for 24 hours.

The next day cut into bite size squares and wrap in wax paper. Store in plastic bag and place in refrigerator

Notes: _____

_____

_____

_____

Recipe 343

CASHEW CARMEL CANDY

Place the following into a vitamix for 5 minutes.

> One half cup of soymilk
> 2 teaspoons of vanilla
> One half cup of sucanant sugar
> 1 cup of maple syrup
> 1 teaspoon of Biosalt
> One large apple or two small (remove core only)

Then pour into a medium size pan. In addition, boil on warm for 50 - 60 minutes, stir occasionally and prepare dish below:

Line a glass dish 8 X 8 inch with parchment paper and add:

One cup of Cashews (chopped) inside dish and set aside.

Start freezer test 45 minutes into boiling.

Freezer test:

Place in a small dish one spoon of the above mixture and place dish in freezer for one minute.

Mixture should be harder at 50 minutes into boiling, repeat freezer test at 55 minutes, mixture will be even harder.

At 60 minutes, mixture should be complete. Pour mixture into glass dish 8 X 8 inch and place in refrigerator uncovered, for 24 hours.

The next day cut into bite size squares and wrap in wax paper. Store in plastic bag and place in refrigerator

Notes: _____

_____

_____

Recipe 344

ROASTED ALMOND CARMEL CANDY

Place the following into a vitamix for 5 minutes.

One half cup of soymilk
2 teaspoons of vanilla
One half cup of sucanant sugar
1 cup of maple syrup
1 teaspoon of Biosalt
One large apple or two small (remove core only)

Then pour into a medium size pan. In addition, boil on warm for 50 - 60 minutes, stir occasionally and prepare dish below:

Line a glass dish 8 X 8 inch with parchment paper and add:

One cup of roasted Almonds (chopped) inside dish and set aside.

Start freezer test 45 minutes into boiling.

Freezer test:

Place in a small dish one spoon of the above mixture and place dish in freezer for one minute.

Mixture should be harder at 50 minutes into boiling, repeat freezer test at 55 minutes, mixture will be even harder.

At 60 minutes, mixture should be complete. Pour mixture into glass dish 8 X 8 inch and place in refrigerator uncovered, for 24 hours.

The next day cut into bite size squares and wrap in wax paper. Store in plastic bag and place in refrigerator

Notes: _____

_____

_____

Recipe 345

LEMON CARMEL CANDY

Place the following into a vitamix for 5 minutes.

　1 - 2 tablespoons lemon rinds
　One half cup of soymilk
　2 teaspoons of vanilla
　One half cup of sucanant sugar
　1 cup of maple syrup
　1 teaspoon of Biosalt
　One large apple or two small (remove core only)

Then pour into a medium size pan. In addition, boil on warm for 50 - 60 minutes, stir occasionally and prepare dish below:

Line a glass dish 8 X 8 inch with parchment paper and add:

One cup of walnuts (chopped) inside dish and set aside.

Start freezer test 45 minutes into boiling.

Freezer test:

Place in a small dish one spoon of the above mixture and place dish in freezer for one minute.

Mixture should be harder at 50 minutes into boiling, repeat freezer test at 55 minutes, mixture will be even harder.

At 60 minutes, mixture should be complete. Pour mixture into glass dish 8 X 8 inch and place in refrigerator uncovered, for 24 hours.

The next day cut into bite size squares and wrap in wax paper. Store in plastic bag and place in refrigerator

Notes:

_____

_____

_____

Recipe 346

ORANGE CARMEL CANDY

Place the following into a vitamix for 5 minutes.

   1 - 2 Tablespoons of Orange rind
   One half cup of soymilk
   2 teaspoons of vanilla
   One half cup of sucanant sugar
   1 cup of maple syrup
   1 teaspoon of Biosalt
   One large apple or two small (remove core only)

Then pour into a medium size pan. In addition, boil on warm for 50 - 60 minutes, stir occasionally and prepare dish below:

Line a glass dish 8 X 8 inch with parchment paper and add:

One cup of walnuts (chopped) inside dish and set aside.

Start freezer test 45 minutes into boiling.

Freezer test:

Place in a small dish one spoon of the above mixture and place dish in freezer for one minute.

Mixture should be harder at 50 minutes into boiling, repeat freezer test at 55 minutes, mixture will be even harder.

At 60 minutes, mixture should be complete. Pour mixture into glass dish 8 X 8 inch and place in refrigerator uncovered, for 24 hours.

The next day cut into bite size squares and wrap in wax paper. Store in plastic bag and place in refrigerator

Notes:

_____

_____

_____

Recipe 347

CAROB CARMEL CANDY

Place the following into a vitamix for 5 minutes.

1 - 2 Tablespoons of Carob
One half cup of soymilk
2 teaspoons of vanilla
One half cup of sucanant sugar
1 cup of maple syrup
1 teaspoon of Biosalt
One large apple or two small (remove core only)

Then pour into a medium size pan. In addition, boil on warm for 50 - 60 minutes, stir occasionally and prepare dish below:

Line a glass dish 8 X 8 inch with parchment paper and add:

One cup of walnuts (chopped) inside dish and set aside.

Start freezer test 45 minutes into boiling.

Freezer test:

Place in a small dish one spoon of the above mixture and place dish in freezer for one minute.

Mixture should be harder at 50 minutes into boiling, repeat freezer test at 55 minutes, mixture will be even harder.

At 60 minutes, mixture should be complete. Pour mixture into glass dish 8 X 8 inch and place in refrigerator uncovered, for 24 hours.

The next day cut into bite size squares and wrap in wax paper. Store in plastic bag and place in refrigerator

Notes: _____

_____

_____

Recipe 348

ROMA CARMEL CANDY

Place the following into a vitamix for 5 minutes.

1 - 2 Tablespoons of Roma
One half cup of soymilk
2 teaspoons of vanilla
One half cup of sucanant sugar
1 cup of maple syrup
1 teaspoon of Biosalt
One large apple or two small (remove core only)

Then pour into a medium size pan. In addition, boil on warm for 50 - 60 minutes, stir occasionally and prepare dish below:

Line a glass dish 8 X 8 inch with parchment paper and add:

One cup of walnuts (chopped) inside dish and set aside.

Start freezer test 45 minutes into boiling.

Freezer test:

Place in a small dish one spoon of the above mixture and place dish in freezer for one minute.

Mixture should be harder at 50 minutes into boiling, repeat freezer test at 55 minutes, mixture will be even harder.

At 60 minutes, mixture should be complete. Pour mixture into glass dish 8 X 8 inch and place in refrigerator uncovered, for 24 hours.

The next day cut into bite size squares and wrap in wax paper. Store in plastic bag and place in refrigerator

Notes:

_____

_____

_____

Recipe 349

PEPPERMINT CARMEL CANDY

Place the following into a vitamix for 5 minutes.

> One half teaspoon of Peppermint oil
> One half cup of soymilk
> 2 teaspoons of vanilla
> One half cup of sucanant sugar
> 1 cup of maple syrup
> 1 teaspoon of Biosalt
> One large apple or two small (remove core only)

Then pour into a medium size pan. In addition, boil on warm for 50 - 60 minutes, stir occasionally and prepare dish below:

Line a glass dish 8 X 8 inch with parchment paper and add:

One cup of walnuts (chopped) inside dish and set aside.

Start freezer test 45 minutes into boiling.

Freezer test:

Place in a small dish one spoon of the above mixture and place dish in freezer for one minute.

Mixture should be harder at 50 minutes into boiling, repeat freezer test at 55 minutes, mixture will be even harder.

At 60 minutes, mixture should be complete. Pour mixture into glass dish 8 X 8 inch and place in refrigerator uncovered, for 24 hours.

The next day cut into bite size squares and wrap in wax paper. Store in plastic bag and place in refrigerator

Notes:

Recipe 350

GINGER CARMEL CANDY

Place the following into a vitamix for 5 minutes.

>   One-half to one teaspoon of Ginger
>   One half cup of soymilk
>   2 teaspoons of vanilla
>   One half cup of sucanant sugar
>   1 cup of maple syrup
>   1 teaspoon of Biosalt
>   One large apple or two small (remove core only)

Then pour into a medium size pan. In addition, boil on warm for 50 - 60 minutes, stir occasionally and prepare dish below:

Line a glass dish 8 X 8 inch with parchment paper and add:

One cup of walnuts (chopped) inside dish and set aside.

Start freezer test 45 minutes into boiling.

Freezer test:

Place in a small dish one spoon of the above mixture and place dish in freezer for one minute.

Mixture should be harder at 50 minutes into boiling, repeat freezer test at 55 minutes, mixture will be even harder.

At 60 minutes, mixture should be complete. Pour mixture into glass dish 8 X 8 inch and place in refrigerator uncovered, for 24 hours.

The next day cut into bite size squares and wrap in wax paper. Store in plastic bag and place in refrigerator

Notes:

_____

_____

_____

Recipe 351 ──────────────────

HERBS AND GARLIC BAKED RICE

The night before place in a glass-baking dish with a lid:

    6 and half cups of water
    4 cups of rice

The next day add:

    1 - 2 tablespoons of Italian seasoning
    One-half chopped onion
    1 - 2 teaspoons of garlic powder or three chopped cloves of garlic
    One half cup of lemon juice
    1 teaspoon of Biosalt

Mix and place in oven.

Bake 250 degrees in oven for 2 hours. Make sure water is gone. In dish, keep lid on dish until cool

Notes: ────────────────────────────
──────────────────────────────
──────────────────────────────

Recipe 352

WALNUT and ALMOND FROSTING

Place into vitamix:

    4 cups of Sucanat sugar

This will make a fine powder.

Then add to a large bowl with the following:

    One fourth cup of soymilk
    2 teaspoons vanilla
    2 cups of almond butter

If mixture is too thick can add more soymilk 1 tablespoon at a time.

If this frosting is for a cake, sprinkle 1 cup of chopped walnuts on top and sides and gently press into cake.

If this frosting is for cookies, sprinkle 1 cup of chopped walnuts and press gently into each cookie

Notes: _____

Recipe 353

PINEAPPLE and LEMON GLAZE

Place 1 cup of Sucanat sugar into vitamix -- this will make sugar into a fine powder.

Then add to a small bowl and mix with the following:

    1 tablespoon of lemon juice
    2 tablespoons of pineapple juice

If using for a cake, -- apply when cake is cool.

If frosting is too thick can add more lemon and pineapple juice 1 tablespoon at a time

Notes: _____

_____

_____

Recipe 354

ROMA TOFU COOKIES

For dough, see Butter cookie recipe # 45

Mix the night before. Wrap and place in refrigerator.

The next day place 3 cups of Sucanat sugar into vitamix.

Make into a fine powder.

Then pour into a large bowl with the following:

  1 Brick or 1 pound of tofu
  1 tablespoon of Roma powder
  4 cups of chopped walnuts

Mix and set aside.

Roll out dough and with a 3 x 3 inch round cookie cutter cut circle into dough.

Place enough mixture into center of circle and fold over. This will look like a half moon.

Press sides together and place in cookie trays lined with parchment paper or cookie matt.

Bake 350 degrees for 20 minutes.

Let cool. Store in freezer

Notes: _____

_____

_____

Recipe 355

CAROB TOFU COOKIES

For dough, see Butter cookie recipe # 45

Mix the night before. Wrap and place in refrigerator.

The next day place 3 cups of Sucanat sugar into vitamix.

Make into a fine powder.

Then pour into a large bowl with the following:

   1 Brick or 1 pound of tofu
   1 tablespoon of carob powder
   4 cups of walnuts (grounded)

Mix and set aside.

Roll out dough and with a 3 x 3 inch round cookie cutter cut circle into dough.

Place enough mixture into center of circle and fold over. This will look like a half moon.

Press sides together and place in cookie trays lined with parchment paper or cookie matt.

Bake 350 degrees for 20 minutes.

Let cool. Store in freezer

Notes: _____

_____

_____

Recipe 356

CINNAMON TOFU COOKIES

For dough, see Butter cookie recipe # 45

Mix the night before. Wrap and place in refrigerator.

The next day place 3 cups of Sucanat sugar into vitamix.

Make into a fine powder.

Then pour into a large bowl with the following:

> 1 Brick or 1 pound of tofu
> 1 tablespoon of cinnamon
> 4 cups of walnuts (grounded)

Mix and set aside.

Roll out dough and with a 3 x 3 inch round cookie cutter cut circle into dough.

Place enough mixture into center of circle and fold over. This will look like a half moon.

Press sides together and place in cookie trays lined with parchment paper or cookie matt.

Bake 350 degrees for 20 minutes.

Let cool. Store in freezer

Notes: _____

_____

_____

Recipe 357

RAISIN TOFU COOKIES

For dough, see Butter cookie recipe # 45

Mix the night before. Wrap and place in refrigerator.

The next day place 3 cups of Sucanat sugar into vitamix.

Make into a fine powder.

Then pour into a large bowl with the following:

   1 Brick or 1 pound of tofu
   2 cups of cleaned raisins

Into vitamix until smooth, pour into the same large bowl with Sucanat sugar and add 2 cups of chopped walnuts

Mix and set aside.

If mixture is too thin, add 1 tablespoon of whole-wheat pastry flour at a time until thick.

Roll out dough and with a 3 x 3 inch round cookie cutter cut circle into dough.

Place enough mixture into center of circle and fold over. This will look like a half moon.

Press sides together and place in cookie trays lined with parchment paper or cookie matt.

Bake 350 degrees for 20 minutes.

Let cool. Store in freezer

Notes: _____

_____

_____

Recipe 358

APRICOT TOFU COOKIES

For dough, see Butter cookie recipe # 45

Mix the night before. Wrap and place in refrigerator.

The next day place 3 cups of Sucanat sugar into vitamix.

Make into a fine powder.

Then pour into a large bowl with the following:

   1 Brick or 1 pound of tofu
   2 cups of apricots minus pits

Into vitamix until smooth, pour into the same large bowl with Sucanat sugar and add 2 cups of chopped walnuts

Mix and set aside.

If mixture is too thin, add 1 tablespoon of whole-wheat pastry flour at a time until thick.

Roll out dough and with a 3 x 3 inch round cookie cutter cut circle into dough.

Place enough mixture into center of circle and fold over. This will look like a half moon.

Press sides together and place in cookie trays lined with parchment paper or cookie matt.

Bake 350 degrees for 20 minutes.

Let cool. Store in freezer

Notes: _____

_____

_____

Recipe 359

DATE TOFU COOKIES

For dough, see Butter cookie recipe # 45

Mix the night before. Wrap and place in refrigerator.

The next day place 3 cups of Sucanat sugar into vitamix.

Make into a fine powder.

Then pour into a large bowl with the following:

    1 Brick or 1 pound of tofu
    2 cups of dates minus pits

Into vitamix until smooth, pour into the same large bowl with Sucanat sugar and add 2 cups of chopped walnuts

Mix and set aside.

If mixture is too thin, add 1 tablespoon of whole-wheat pastry flour at a time until thick.

Roll out dough and with a 3 x 3 inch round cookie cutter cut circle into dough.

Place enough mixture into center of circle and fold over. This will look like a half moon.

Press sides together and place in cookie trays lined with parchment paper or cookie matt.

Bake 350 degrees for 20 minutes.

Let cool. Store in freezer

Notes: _____

_____

_____

Recipe 360 _____

CRANBERRIE TOFU COOKIES

For dough, see Butter cookie recipe # 45

Mix the night before. Wrap and place in refrigerator.

The next day place 3 cups of Sucanat sugar into vitamix.

Make into a fine powder.

Then pour into a large bowl with the following:

    1 Brick or 1 pound of tofu
    2 cups of cranberries

Into vitamix and blend until smooth, pour into the same large bowl with Sucanat sugar and add 2 cups of chopped walnuts

Mix and set aside.

If mixture is too thin, add 1 tablespoon of whole-wheat pastry flour at a time until thick.

Roll out dough and with a 3 x 3 inch round cookie cutter cut circle into dough.

Place enough mixture into center of circle and fold over. This will look like a half moon.

Press sides together and place in cookie trays lined with parchment paper or cookie matt.

Bake 350 degrees for 20 minutes.

Let cool. Store in freezer

Notes: _____
_____
_____

Recipe 361

SPICE TOFU COOKIES

For dough see Butter cookie recipe # 45

Mix the night before. Wrap and place in refrigerator.

   The next day place 3 cups of Sucanat sugar into vitamix
   Make into a fine powder.

Then pour into a large bowl with the following:

   One half teaspoon of clove powder
   One half teaspoon of ginger powder
   One half teaspoon of cinnamon powder
   1 Brick or 1 pound of tofu
   into vitamix and blend until smooth, pour into the same large bowl with
   Sucanat sugar and add
   4 cups of grounded walnuts
   Mix and set aside.

If mixture is too thin add 1 tablespoon of whole wheat pastry flour at a time until thick.

Roll out dough and with a 3 x 3 inch round cookie cutter cut circle into dough.

Place enough mixture into center of circle and fold over. This will look like a half moon.

Press sides together and place in cookie trays lined with parchment paper or cookie mat.

Bake 350 degrees for 20 minutes.

Let cool. Store in freezer.

Notes: _____

_____

_____

Recipe 362

PAPAYA TOFU COOKIES

For dough, see Butter cookie recipe # 45

Mix the night before. Wrap and place in refrigerator.

The next day place 3 cups of Sucanat sugar into vitamix.

Make into a fine powder.

Then pour into a large bowl with the following:

    1 Brick or 1 pound of tofu
    2 cups of papaya

Into vitamix and blend until smooth, pour into the same large bowl with Sucanat sugar and add 2 cups of chopped walnuts

Mix and set aside.

If mixture is too thin, add 1 tablespoon of whole-wheat pastry flour at a time until thick.

Roll out dough and with a 3 x 3 inch round cookie cutter cut circle into dough.

Place enough mixture into center of circle and fold over. This will look like a half moon.

Press sides together and place in cookie trays lined with parchment paper or cookie matt.

Bake 350 degrees for 20 minutes.

Let cool. Store in freezer

Notes: _____

_____

_____

Recipe 363 —————————————————————

COCONUT TOFU COOKIES

For dough, see Butter cookie recipe # 45

Mix the night before. Wrap and place in refrigerator.

The next day place 3 cups of Sucanat sugar into vitamix.

Make into a fine powder.

Then pour into a large bowl with the following:

   1 Brick or 1 pound of tofu
   2 cups of coconut flour

Into vitamix and blend until smooth, pour into the same large bowl with Sucanat sugar and add 2 cups of chopped walnuts

Mix and set aside.

If mixture is too thin, add 1 tablespoon of whole-wheat pastry flour at a time until thick.

Roll out dough and with a 3 x 3 inch round cookie cutter cut circle into dough.

Place enough mixture into center of circle and fold over. This will look like a half moon.

Press sides together and place in cookie trays lined with parchment paper or cookie matt.

Bake 350 degrees for 20 minutes.

Let cool. Store in freezer

Notes: —————————————————————————
—————————————————————————————
—————————————————————————————

Recipe 364

LEMON TOFU COOKIES

For dough, see Butter cookie recipe # 45

Mix the night before. Wrap and place in refrigerator.

The next day place 3 cups of Sucanat sugar into vitamix.

Make into a fine powder.

Then pour into a large bowl with the following:

    1 Brick or 1 pound of tofu
    1 tablespoon of lemon rind

Into vitamix and blend until smooth, pour into the same large bowl with Sucanat sugar and add 4 cups of chopped walnuts

Mix and set aside.

If mixture is too thin, add 1 tablespoon of whole-wheat pastry flour at a time until thick.

Roll out dough and with a 3 x 3 inch round cookie cutter cut circle into dough.

Place enough mixture into center of circle and fold over. This will look like a half moon.

Press sides together and place in cookie trays lined with parchment paper or cookie matt.

Bake 350 degrees for 20 minutes.

Let cool. Store in freezer

Notes: _____

_____

_____

Recipe 365

ORANGE TOFU COOKIES

For dough, see Butter cookie recipe # 45

Mix the night before. Wrap and place in refrigerator.

The next day place 3 cups of Sucanat sugar into vitamix.

Make into a fine powder.

Then pour into a large bowl with the following:

>   1 Brick or 1 pound of tofu
>   1 tablespoon of orange rind

Into vitamix and blend until smooth, pour into the same large bowl with Sucanat sugar and add 4 cups of chopped walnuts

Mix and set aside.

If mixture is too thin, add 1 tablespoon of whole-wheat pastry flour at a time until thick.

Roll out dough and with a 3 x 3 inch round cookie cutter cut circle into dough.

Place enough mixture into center of circle and fold over. This will look like a half moon.

Press sides together and place in cookie trays lined with parchment paper or cookie matt.

Bake 350 degrees for 20 minutes.

Let cool. Store in freezer

Notes: _____

_____

_____

Recipe 366

PINEAPPLE TOFU COOKIES

For dough, see Butter cookie recipe # 45

Mix the night before. Wrap and place in refrigerator.

The next day place 3 cups of Sucanat sugar into vitamix.

Make into a fine powder.

Then pour into a large bowl with the following:

    1 Brick or 1 pound of tofu
    2 cups of pineapple

Into vitamix and blend until smooth, pour into the same large bowl with Sucanat sugar and add 2 cups of chopped walnuts

Mix and set aside.

If mixture is too thin, add 1 tablespoon of whole-wheat pastry flour at a time until thick.

Roll out dough and with a 3 x 3 inch round cookie cutter cut circle into dough.

Place enough mixture into center of circle and fold over. This will look like a half moon.

Press sides together and place in cookie trays lined with parchment paper or cookie matt.

Bake 350 degrees for 20 minutes.

Let cool. Store in freezer

Notes: _____
_____
_____

Recipe 367

BLACK BEAN SOUP

Place in a large pan all the following and boil for 5 minutes -- stir.

Four onions chopped
3 teaspoonfuls of cumin
Eight cloves of garlic
Two stalks of celery chopped
One cups of cilantro chopped
6 tablespoons of hot sauce
2 tablespoons chili powder
2 tablespoons of maple syrup
2 tablespoons of Braggs Ammino
2 tablespoons of Biosalt
Three baked potatoes remove skin and cut into small squares

Add 24 ounces of cooked black beans

Then add 11 cups of water.

Bring to a boil and turn to low. Boil 30 minutes. Place extra into 12-ounce jars and freeze

Notes: _____

_____

_____

Recipe 368

LEMON COCONUT COOKIES

Place the following into vitamix:

    Two cups maple syrup
    One teaspoon Biosalt
    Two cups Almond Butter
    Five teaspoons lemon rind
    ½ c of tofu

Mix and pour into a large bowl

Add two and ½ cups dried coconut

Four cups sifted whole-pastry flour

Mix and form cookies on tray

(one to two spoons mixture)

Place on trays lined with cookie mat

Bake 375 degrees for 13 to 15 minutes

Notes: _____

_____

_____

Recipe 369

CHERRY SUGAR COOKIES

Place into vitamix the following:

1 cup of cherries (minus pits)
2 cups of maple syrup
2 cups of sucanant sugar
2 cups of almond butter
2 teaspoons of vanilla
1 teaspoon of Biosalt
½ cup of Tofu

Mix and pour into a large bowl and add

5 cups of whole-wheat pastry flour sifted

Mix and form into cookies on trays lined with parchment paper or cookie mat.

Bake 375 degrees 15 minutes

Helpful hints:

Mix dough the night before
Cover bowl and place in refrigerator

Notes: _____

_____

_____

Recipe 370 ————————————————————

ORANGE SUGAR COOKIES

Place into vitamix the following:

 5 teaspoons of orange rind
 2 cups of maple syrup
 2 cups of sucanant sugar
 2 cups of almond butter
 2 teaspoons of vanilla
 1 teaspoon of Biosalt
 ½ cup of Tofu

Mix and pour into a large bowl and add

 5 cups of whole-wheat pastry flour sifted

Mix and form into cookies on trays lined with parchment paper or cookie mat.

Bake 375 degrees 15 minutes

Helpful hints:

 Mix dough the night before
 Cover bowl and place in refrigerator

Notes: ———————————————————————

———————————————————————

———————————————————————

Recipe 371

RAISIN SUGAR COOKIES

Place into vitamix the following:

 1 cup of clean raisins
 2 cups of maple syrup
 2 cups of sucanant sugar
 2 cups of almond butter
 2 teaspoons of vanilla
 1 teaspoon of Biosalt
 ½ cup of Tofu

Mix and pour into a large bowl and add

 5 cups of whole-wheat pastry flour sifted

Mix and form into cookies on trays lined with parchment paper or cookie mat.

Bake 375 degrees 15 minutes

Helpful hints:

 Mix dough the night before
 Cover bowl and place in refrigerator

Notes: _____
 _____
 _____

Recipe 372

ROMA SUGAR COOKIES

Place into vitamix the following:

  2 tablespoons of Pero or Roma powder
  2 cups of maple syrup
  2 cups of sucanant sugar
  2 cups of almond butter
  2 teaspoons of vanilla
  1 teaspoon of Biosalt
  ½ cup of Tofu

Mix and pour into a large bowl and add

  5 cups of whole-wheat pastry flour sifted

Mix and form into cookies on trays lined with parchment paper or cookie mat.

Bake 375 degrees 15 minutes

Helpful hints:

  Mix dough the night before
  Cover bowl and place in refrigerator

Notes: _____

_____

_____

Recipe 373

APPLE SUGAR COOKIES

Place into vitamix the following:

    1 cup of apples (remove core only)
    2 cups of maple syrup
    2 cups of sucanant sugar
    2 cups of almond butter
    2 teaspoons of vanilla
    1 teaspoon of Biosalt
    ½ cup of Tofu

Mix and pour into a large bowl and add

    5 cups of whole-wheat pastry flour sifted

Mix and form into cookies on trays lined with parchment paper or cookie mat.

Bake 375 degrees 15 minutes

Helpful hints:

    Mix dough the night before
    Cover bowl and place in refrigerator

Notes: _____

_____

_____

Recipe 374

CAROB SUGAR COOKIES

Place into vitamix the following:

    2 tablespoons of carob powder
    2 cups of maple syrup
    2 cups of sucanant sugar
    2 cups of almond butter
    2 teaspoons of vanilla
    1 teaspoon of Biosalt
    ½ cup of Tofu

Mix and pour into a large bowl and add

    5 cups of whole-wheat pastry flour sifted

Mix and form into cookies on trays lined with parchment paper or cookie mat.

Bake 375 degrees 15 minutes

Helpful hints:

    Mix dough the night before
    Cover bowl and place in refrigerator

Notes: _____

_____

_____

Recipe 375 ————————————

PEPPERMINT SUGAR COOKIES

Place into vitamix the following:

¼ teaspoon of peppermint oil
2 cups of maple syrup
2 cups of sucanant sugar
2 cups of almond butter
2 teaspoons of vanilla
1 teaspoon of biosalt

Mix and pour into a large bowl and add

5 cups of whole wheat pastry flour sifted

Mix and form into cookies on trays lined with parchment paper or cookie mat.

Bake 375 degrees 15 minutes

Helpful hints:

Mix dough the night before
cover bowl and place in refrigerator

Notes: ————————————————

————————————————

————————————————

Recipe 376 _____

BLUEBERRY SUGAR COOKIES

Place into vitamix the following:

    1 cup of cleaned blueberries
    2 cups of maple syrup
    2 cups of sucanant sugar
    2 cups of almond butter
    2 teaspoons of vanilla
    1 teaspoon of biosalt

Mix and pour into a large bowl and add

    5 cups of whole wheat pastry flour sifted

Mix and form into cookies on trays lined with parchment paper or cookie mat.

Bake 375 degrees 15 minutes

Helpful hints:

    Mix dough the night before
    cover bowl and place in refrigerator

Notes: _____

_____

_____

Recipe 377 —————————————————

DATE SUGAR COOKIES

Place into vitamix the following:

    1 cup of cleaned dates
    2 cups of maple syrup
    2 cups of sucanant sugar
    2 cups of almond butter
    2 teaspoons of vanilla
    1 teaspoon of Biosalt
    ½ cup of Tofu

Mix and pour into a large bowl and add

    5 cups of whole-wheat pastry flour sifted

Mix and form into cookies on trays lined with parchment paper or cookie mat.

Bake 375 degrees 15 minutes

Helpful hints:

    Mix dough the night before
    Cover bowl and place in refrigerator

Notes: _____
            _____
            _____

Recipe 378 _____

PINEAPPLE SUGAR COOKIES

Place into vitamix the following:

    1 cup of pineapple
    2 cups of maple syrup
    2 cups of sucanant sugar
    2 cups of almond butter
    2 teaspoons of vanilla
    1 teaspoon of Biosalt
    ½ cup of Tofu

Mix and pour into a large bowl and add

    5 cups of whole-wheat pastry flour sifted

Mix and form into cookies on trays lined with parchment paper or cookie mat.

Bake 375 degrees 15 minutes

Helpful hints:

    Mix dough the night before
    Cover bowl and place in refrigerator

Notes: _____

_____

_____

Recipe 379 —————————————————————

PLUM SUGAR COOKIES

Place into vitamix the following:

> 1 cup of plums (minus pit)
> 2 cups of maple syrup
> 2 cups of sucanant sugar
> 2 cups of almond butter
> 2 teaspoons of vanilla
> 1 teaspoon of Biosalt
> ½ cup of Tofu

Mix and pour into a large bowl and add

> 5 cups of whole-wheat pastry flour sifted

Mix and form into cookies on trays lined with parchment paper or cookie mat.

Bake 375 degrees 15 minutes

Helpful hints:

> Mix dough the night before
> Cover bowl and place in refrigerator

Notes: _____

_____

_____

Recipe 380

PEACH SUGAR COOKIES

Place into vitamix the following:

    1 cup of peach (minus pit)
    2 cups of maple syrup
    2 cups of sucanant sugar
    2 cups of almond butter
    2 teaspoons of vanilla
    1 teaspoon of Biosalt
    ½ cup of Tofu

Mix and pour into a large bowl and add

    5 cups of whole-wheat pastry flour sifted

Mix and form into cookies on trays lined with parchment paper or cookie mat.

Bake 375 degrees 15 minutes

Helpful hints:

    Mix dough the night before
    Cover bowl and place in refrigerator

Notes: _____

_____

_____

Recipe 381

APRICOT SUGAR COOKIES

Place into vitamix the following:

 1 cup of apricots (minus pit)
 2 cups of maple syrup
 2 cups of sucanant sugar
 2 cups of almond butter
 2 teaspoons of vanilla
 1 teaspoon of Biosalt
 ½ cup of Tofu

Mix and pour into a large bowl and add

 5 cups of whole-wheat pastry flour sifted

Mix and form into cookies on trays lined with parchment paper or cookie mat.

Bake 375 degrees 15 minutes

Helpful hints:

 Mix dough the night before
 Cover bowl and place in refrigerator

Notes: _____

_____

_____

Recipe 382

NECTARINE SUGAR COOKIES

Place into vitamix the following:

    1 cup of nectarines (minus pit)
    2 cups of maple syrup
    2 cups of sucanant sugar
    2 cups of almond butter
    2 teaspoons of vanilla
    1 teaspoon of Biosalt
    ½ cup of Tofu

Mix and pour into a large bowl and add

    5 cups of whole-wheat pastry flour sifted

Mix and form into cookies on trays lined with parchment paper or cookie mat.

Bake 375 degrees 15 minutes

Helpful hints:

    Mix dough the night before
    Cover bowl and place in refrigerator

Notes: _____

                _____

                _____

Recipe 383

CRANBERRY SUGAR COOKIES

Place into vitamix the following:

    1 cup of cranberry
    2 cups of maple syrup
    2 cups of sucanant sugar
    2 cups of almond butter
    2 teaspoons of vanilla
    1 teaspoon of Biosalt
    ½ cup of Tofu

Mix and pour into a large bowl and add

    5 cups of whole-wheat pastry flour sifted

Mix and form into cookies on trays lined with parchment paper or cookie mat.

Bake 375 degrees 15 minutes

Helpful hints:

    Mix dough the night before
    Cover bowl and place in refrigerator

Notes: _____

*Recipe 384*_____

PUMPKIN SUGAR COOKIES

Place into vitamix the following:

    1 cup of pumpkin
    2 cups of maple syrup
    2 cups of sucanant sugar
    2 cups of almond butter
    2 teaspoons of vanilla
    1 teaspoon of Biosalt
    ½ cup of Tofu

Mix and pour into a large bowl and add

    5 cups of whole-wheat pastry flour sifted

Mix and form into cookies on trays lined with parchment paper or cookie mat.

Bake 375 degrees 15 minutes

Helpful hints:

    Mix dough the night before
    Cover bowl and place in refrigerator

Notes: _____

               _____

               _____

Recipe 385

COCONUT CAROB CARMEL CANDY

Place the following into vitamix for 5 minutes:

> One to two tablespoons of carob powder
> One half cup of soymilk
> Two teaspoons of vanilla
> One and half cups of maple syrup
> One teaspoon of Biosalt
> One large apple or two small - remove core only

Then pour into a medium size pan and boil on warm for 50 to 60 minutes, stir occasionally and prepare dish. Line a glass dish 8 x 8 inch with parchment paper and add one cup of coconut flour inside dish and set aside.

Start freezer test 45 minutes into boiling.

Freezer test:

Place in a small dish one spoon of the above mixture and place dish in freezer for one minute.

Mixture should be harder, at 50 minutes into boiling repeat freezer test.

At 55 minutes, mixture will be even harder at 60 minutes.

Mixture will be complete.

Pour entire mixture into glass dish 8 x 8 inches.

Place in refrigerator for 24 hours uncovered.

The next day cut into bite size squares. Both sides and ends should be covered in coconut flour-- wrap each square in wax paper, place in bag into refrigerator

Frederick Mickel Huck

Notes:

_____

_____

_____

Recipe 386

COCONUT LEMON CARMEL CANDY

Place the following into vitamix for 5 minutes:

One to two tablespoons of lemon rind
One half cup of soymilk
Two teaspoons of vanilla
One and half cups of maple syrup
One teaspoon of Biosalt
One large apple or two small - remove core only

Then pour into a medium size pan and boil on warm for 50 to 60 minutes, stir occasionally and prepare dish. Line a glass dish 8 x 8 inch with parchment paper and add one cup of coconut flour inside dish and set aside.

Start freezer test 45 minutes into boiling.

Freezer test:

Place in a small dish one spoon of the above mixture and place dish in freezer for one minute.

Mixture should be harder, at 50 minutes into boiling repeat freezer test.

At 55 minutes, mixture will be even harder at 60 minutes.

Mixture will be complete.

Pour entire mixture into glass dish 8 x 8 inches.

Place in refrigerator for 24 hours uncovered.

The next day cut into bite size squares. Both sides and ends should be covered in coconut flour-- wrap each square in wax paper, place in bag into refrigerator

Notes:

_____

_____

_____

Recipe 387

COCONUT CINNAMON CARMEL CANDY

Place the following into vitamix for 5 minutes:

One tablespoon cinnamon
One half cup of soymilk
Two teaspoons of vanilla
One and half cups of maple syrup
One teaspoon of Biosalt
One large apple or two small - remove core only

Then pour into a medium size pan and boil on warm for 50 to 60 minutes, stir occasionally and prepare dish. Line a glass dish 8 x 8 inch with parchment paper and add one cup of coconut flour inside dish and set aside.

Start freezer test 45 minutes into boiling.

Freezer test:

Place in a small dish one spoon of the above mixture and place dish in freezer for one minute.

Mixture should be harder, at 50 minutes into boiling repeat freezer test.

At 55 minutes, mixture will be even harder at 60 minutes.

Mixture will be complete.

Pour entire mixture into glass dish 8 x 8 inches.

Place in refrigerator for 24 hours uncovered.

The next day cut into bite size squares. Both sides and ends should be covered in coconut flour-- wrap each square in wax paper, place in bag into refrigerator

Notes:

_____

_____

_____

Recipe 388

COCONUT ORANGE CARMEL CANDY

Place the following into vitamix for 5 minutes:

One to two tablespoons of orange rind
One half cup of soymilk
Two teaspoons of vanilla
One and half cups of maple syrup
One teaspoon of Biosalt
One large apple or two small - remove core only

Then pour into a medium size pan and boil on warm for 50 to 60 minutes, stir occasionally and prepare dish. Line a glass dish 8 x 8 inch with parchment paper and add one cup of coconut flour inside dish and set aside.

Start freezer test 45 minutes into boiling.

Freezer test:

Place in a small dish one spoon of the above mixture and place dish in freezer for one minute.

Mixture should be harder, at 50 minutes into boiling repeat freezer test.

At 55 minutes, mixture will be even harder at 60 minutes.

Mixture will be complete.

Pour entire mixture into glass dish 8 x 8 inches.

Place in refrigerator for 24 hours uncovered.

The next day cut into bite size squares. Both sides and ends should be covered in coconut flour-- wrap each square in wax paper, place in bag into refrigerator

Notes:

_____

_____

_____

Recipe 389

COCONUT PEPPERMINT CARMEL CANDY

Place the following into vitamix for 5 minutes:

½ teaspoon of liquid peppermint
One half cup of soymilk
Two teaspoons of vanilla
One and half cups of maple syrup
One teaspoon of Biosalt
One large apple or two small - remove core only

Then pour into a medium size pan and boil on warm for 50 to 60 minutes, stir occasionally and prepare dish. Line a glass dish 8 x 8 inch with parchment paper and add one cup of coconut flour inside dish and set aside.

Start freezer test 45 minutes into boiling.

Freezer test:

Place in a small dish one spoon of the above mixture and place dish in freezer for one minute.

Mixture should be harder, at 50 minutes into boiling repeat freezer test.

At 55 minutes, mixture will be even harder at 60 minutes.

Mixture will be complete.

Pour entire mixture into glass dish 8 x 8 inches.

Place in refrigerator for 24 hours uncovered.

The next day cut into bite size squares. Both sides and ends should be covered in coconut flour-- wrap each square in wax paper, place in bag into refrigerator

Frederick Mickel Huck

Notes:

_____

_____

_____

Recipe 390

COCONUT PERO CARMEL CANDY

Place the following into vitamix for 5 minutes:

    One to two tablespoons of Pero
    One half cup of soymilk
    Two teaspoons of vanilla
    One and half cups of maple syrup
    One teaspoon of Biosalt
    One large apple or two small - remove core only

Then pour into a medium size pan and boil on warm for 50 to 60 minutes, stir occasionally and prepare dish. Line a glass dish 8 x 8 inch with parchment paper and add one cup of coconut flour inside dish and set aside.

Start freezer test 45 minutes into boiling.

Freezer test:

Place in a small dish one spoon of the above mixture and place dish in freezer for one minute.

Mixture should be harder, at 50 minutes into boiling repeat freezer test.

At 55 minutes, mixture will be even harder at 60 minutes.

Mixture will be complete.

Pour entire mixture into glass dish 8 x 8 inches.

Place in refrigerator for 24 hours uncovered.

The next day cut into bite size squares. Both sides and ends should be covered in coconut flour-- wrap each square in wax paper, place in bag into refrigerator

Notes: _____

_____

_____

Recipe 391

COCONUT GINGER CARMEL CANDY

Place the following into vitamix for 5 minutes:

½ to One teaspoon ginger
One half cup soymilk
Two teaspoons vanilla
One and half cups maple syrup
One teaspoon Biosalt
One large apple or two small - remove core only

Then pour into a medium size pan and boil on warm for 50 to 60 minutes, stir occasionally and prepare dish. Line a glass dish 8 x 8 inch with parchment paper and add one cup of coconut flour inside dish and set aside.

Start freezer test 45 minutes into boiling.

Freezer test:

Place in a small dish one spoon of the above mixture and place dish in freezer for one minute.

Mixture should be harder, at 50 minutes into boiling repeat freezer test.

At 55 minutes, mixture will be even harder at 60 minutes.

Mixture will be complete.

Pour entire mixture into glass dish 8 x 8 inches.

Place in refrigerator for 24 hours uncovered.

The next day cut into bite size squares. Both sides and ends should be covered in coconut flour-- wrap each square in wax paper, place in bag into refrigerator

Notes:

_____

_____

_____

Recipe 392

DATE OATMEAL COOKIES

Place the following into vitamix:

    One cup of dates (minus pit)
    Two teaspoons vanilla
    Two cups maple syrup
    ½ teaspoon Biosalt
    2 cups Almond Butter

Mix and pour into a large bowl

    Add two cups of Oatmeal Flour
    Four cups sifted whole-pastry flour

Mix and form cookies on tray

(one to two spoons mixture)

Place on trays lined with cookie mat

Bake 325 degrees for 20 minutes

Notes: _____

_____

_____

Recipe 393 ⎯⎯⎯⎯⎯⎯⎯⎯⎯⎯⎯⎯⎯⎯⎯⎯⎯⎯⎯

RAISIN OATMEAL COOKIES

Place the following into vitamix:

One cup of raisins
Two teaspoons vanilla
Two cups maple syrup
½ teaspoon Biosalt
2 cups Almond Butter

Mix and pour into a large bowl

Add two cups of Oatmeal Flour
Four cups sifted whole-pastry flour

Mix and form cookies on tray

(one to two spoons mixture)

Place on trays lined with cookie mat

Bake 325 degrees for 20 minutes

Notes: ⎯⎯⎯⎯⎯⎯⎯⎯⎯⎯⎯⎯⎯⎯⎯⎯⎯⎯
⎯⎯⎯⎯⎯⎯⎯⎯⎯⎯⎯⎯⎯⎯⎯⎯⎯⎯⎯⎯⎯
⎯⎯⎯⎯⎯⎯⎯⎯⎯⎯⎯⎯⎯⎯⎯⎯⎯⎯⎯⎯⎯

Recipe 394

WALNUT DATE COOKIES

Place the following into vitamix:

    One teaspoon vanilla
    Three cups maple syrup
    One teaspoon Biosalt
    One teaspoon Almond Butter
    Two cups of Dates (minus pit)

Mix and pour into a large bowl

    Add six cups chopped walnuts
    Four cups sifted whole-pastry flour

Mix and form cookies on tray

(one to two spoons mixture)

Place on trays lined with cookie mat

Bake 325 degrees for 25 minutes

Notes: _____

_____

_____

Recipe 395

WALNUT LEMON COOKIES

Place the following into vitamix:

> One teaspoon vanilla
> Three cups maple syrup
> One teaspoon Biosalt
> One teaspoon Almond Butter
> Five teaspoons of lemon rind

Mix and pour into a large bowl

> Add six cups chopped walnuts
> Four cups sifted whole-pastry flour

Mix and form cookies on tray

(one to two spoons mixture)

Place on trays lined with cookie mat

Bake 325 degrees for 25 minutes

Notes: _____

_____

_____

Recipe 396

WALNUT RAISIN COOKIES

Place the following into vitamix:

>   One teaspoon vanilla
>   Three cups maple syrup
>   One teaspoon Biosalt
>   One teaspoon Almond Butter
>   Two cups cleaned raisins

Mix and pour into a large bowl

>   Add six cups chopped walnuts
>   Four cups sifted whole-pastry flour

Mix and form cookies on tray

(one to two spoons mixture)

Place on trays lined with cookie mat

Bake 325 degrees for 25 minutes

Notes: _____

_____

_____

Recipe 397 _____

WALNUT ORANGE COOKIES

Place the following into vitamix:

   One teaspoon vanilla
   Three cups maple syrup
   One teaspoon Biosalt
   One teaspoon Almond Butter
   Five teaspoons orange rind

Mix and pour into a large bowl

   Add six cups chopped walnuts
   Four cups sifted whole-pastry flour

Mix and form cookies on tray

(one to two spoons mixture)

Place on trays lined with cookie mat

Bake 325 degrees for 25 minutes

Notes: _____

_____

_____

Recipe 398

WALNUT CHERRY COOKIES

Place the following into vitamix:

    One teaspoon vanilla
    Three cups maple syrup
    One teaspoon Biosalt
    One teaspoon Almond Butter
    Two cups cherries (minus pit)

Mix and pour into a large bowl

    Add six cups chopped walnuts
    Four cups sifted whole-pastry flour

Mix and form cookies on tray

(one to two spoons mixture)

Place on trays lined with cookie mat

Bake 325 degrees for 25 minutes

Notes: _____
_____
_____

Recipe 399————————————————————

COCONUT DATE COOKIES

Place the following into vitamix:

    Two cups maple syrup
    One teaspoon Biosalt
    Two cups Almond Butter
    One cup dates (minus pit)

Mix and pour into a large bowl

    Add two cups dried coconut
    Four cups sifted whole-pastry flour

Mix and form cookies on tray

(one to two spoons mixture)

Place on trays lined with cookie mat

Bake 375 degrees for 13 to 15 minutes

Notes: _____

              _____

              _____

*Recipe 400*_____

COCONUT CHERRY COOKIES

Place the following into vitamix:

    Two cups maple syrup
    One teaspoon Biosalt
    Two cups Almond Butter
    One cup of cherries (minus pit)

Mix and pour into a large bowl

    Add two and ½ cups dried coconut
    Four cups sifted whole-pastry flour

Mix and form cookies on tray

(one to two spoons mixture)

Place on trays lined with cookie mat

Bake 375 degrees for 13 to 15 minutes

Notes: _____

_____

_____

Recipe 401 _____

COCONUT RAISIN COOKIES

Place the following into vitamix:

    Two cups maple syrup
    One teaspoon Biosalt
    Two cups Almond Butter
    One cup cleaned raisins

Mix and pour into a large bowl

    Add two cups dried coconut
    Four cups sifted whole-pastry flour

Mix and form cookies on tray

(one to two spoons mixture)

Place on trays lined with cookie mat

Bake 375 degrees for 13 to 15 minutes

Notes: _____

_____

_____

Recipe 402

ONION DRY ROASTED NUTS

Mix in a large bowl the following:

    4 cups of walnuts
    4 cups of almonds
    4 cups of pecans

Spray and coat with Braggs and mix well.

Then add:

    2 tablespoons of onion powder
    1 tablespoon of Biosalt

Spray again with Braggs. Mix and coat well.

In addition, add 4 cups of Puffed corn and mix well.

Place on tray lined with cookie mat.

Bake at 200 degrees for 12 hours overnight or until dry

Notes: _____

_____

_____

Recipe 403

GARLIC DRY ROASTED NUTS

Mix in a large bowl the following:

    4 cups of walnuts

    4 cups of almonds

    4 cups of pecans

Spray and coat with Braggs and mix well.

Then add:

    2 tablespoons of garlic powder

    1 tablespoon of Biosalt

Spray again with Braggs. Mix and coat well.

In addition, add 4 cups of Puffed corn and mix well.

Place on tray lined with cookie mat.

Bake at 200 degrees for 12 hours overnight or until dry

Notes: _____

_____

_____

Recipe 404

HABANERO DRIED ROASTED NUTS

Place in a vitamix the following:

>   12 – 15 Habanero peppers
>   One half cup of maple syrup
>   One third cup of lemon juice

pour into a large bowl and add the following:

>   4 cups of walnuts
>   4 cups of almonds
>   4 cups of pecans

Mix and Spray and with Braggs

Then add

>   1 tablespoon of garlic powder.
>   2 tablespoons of biosalt
>   1 tablespoon of chili powder
>   1 tablespoon of paprika
>   1 tablespoon of onion powder

spray again with Braggs.   Mix and coat well and add 4 cups of Puffed corn.

Mix well.

Place on tray lined with cookie mat

Bake at 200 degrees for 12 hours overnight or until crisp.

Notes: _____

_____

_____

Recipe 405

CAYENNE DRY ROASTED NUTS

Mix in a large bowl the following:

    4 cups of walnuts

    4 cups of almonds

    4 cups of pecans

Spray and coat with Braggs and mix well.

Then add:

    One half cup of maple syrup

    1 tablespoon of Biosalt

    3 - 5 tablespoons of Cayenne pepper

Spray again with Braggs. Mix and coat well.

In addition, add 4 cups of Puffed corn and mix well.

Place on tray lined with cookie mat.

Bake at 200 degrees for 12 hours overnight or until dry

Notes: _____

_____

_____

Recipe 406

BLACK BEAN RICE

For rice, see recipe #5

Mix the night before.

In a small pan boil on low, the following for 10 to 20 minutes or until most of the liquid is gone.

 1 cup of water or 1 cup of pineapple juice.
 2 tablespoons of Braggs
 1 teaspoon Biosalt
 One half cup of cilantro
 One onion cut small
 Two stalks of celery cut small

Boil and stir then add 12 ounces of cooked black beans.

Mix and add entire mixture to cooked rice.

Place into 6-ounce cups and freeze until needed

Notes: _____

_____

_____

Recipe 407

SALTED - HABANERO DRY ROASTED NUTS

Place in a vitamix the following:

One third cup of maple syrup
One third cup lemon juice
12 Havenaro peppers

Mix and pour into a large bowl with the following:

4 cups of walnuts
4 cups of almonds
4 cups of pecans

Mix and Spray with Braggs. Coat all nuts and add 2 tablespoons of Biosalt.

Spray again with Braggs.

Mix and then add 4 cups of Puffed corn.

And then mix and place on tray lined with cookie mat.

Bake in oven for 12 hours overnight or more

Notes: _____

_____

_____

Recipe 408

MAPLE SYRUP DRY ROASTED NUTS

Mix in a large bowl the following:

   4 cups of walnuts
   4 cups of almonds
   4 cups of pecans

Spray and coat with Braggs. -- mix well.

Then add 1 tablespoon of Biosalt

Mix again and spry with Braggs, then add

   1 cup of maple syrup

Mix and spray again with Braggs

Then add 4 cups of Puffed corn.

In addition, mix until all ingredients are coated.

Place on tray lined with cookie mat.

Bake 200 degrees in oven for 12 hours overnight or until dry

Notes: _____

_____

_____

Recipe 409

CAROB MACAROONS

Mix the following the night before and place in refrigerator covered.

Place in a large bowl the following:

One half cup of carob powder
6 cups of maple syrup
4 cups of coconut
1 teaspoon of Biosalt
2 teaspoons of almond butter

Mix and add 5 cups of Whole-wheat pastry flour sifted

Place on trays 2 spoons of the mixture at a time to form cookie into a circle.

All trays lined with cookie mat. Alternatively, parchment paper.

Bake 350 degrees for 25 minutes

Notes: _____

_____

_____

Recipe 410

LEMON MACAROONS

Mix the following the night before and place in refrigerator covered.

Place in a large bowl the following:

> 1 cup of lemon rind
> 6 cups of maple syrup
> 4 cups of coconut
> 1 teaspoon of Biosalt
> 2 teaspoons of almond butter

Mix and add 5 cups of Whole-wheat pastry flour sifted

Place on trays 2 spoons of the mixture form cookie into a circle.

All trays lined with cookie mat. Alternatively, parchment paper.

Bake 325 degrees for 25 minutes

Notes: _____

_____

_____

Recipe 411 _____

ROMA MACAROONS

Mix the following the night before and place in refrigerator covered.

Place in a large bowl the following:

> One half cup of Roma
> 6 cups of maple syrup
> 4 cups of coconut
> 1 teaspoon of Biosalt
> 2 teaspoons of almond butter

Mix and add 5 cups of Whole-wheat pastry flour sifted

Place on trays 2 spoons of the mixture form cookie into a circle.

All trays lined with cookie mat. Or parchment paper.

Bake 325 degrees for 25 minutes

Notes: _____
_____
_____

Recipe 412

ORANGE MACAROONS

Mix the following the night before and place in refrigerator covered.

Place in a large bowl the following:

> One cup of orange rind
> 6 cups of maple syrup
> 4 cups of coconut
> 1 teaspoon of Biosalt
> 2 teaspoons of almond butter

Mix and add 5 cups of Whole-wheat pastry flour sifted

Place on trays 2 spoons of the mixture form cookie into a circle.

All trays lined with cookie mat. Or parchment paper.

Bake 325 degrees for 25 minutes

Notes: _____

_____

_____

Recipe 413 ─────────────

PEPPERMINT FROSTING

Mix the following in a bowl:

    3 tablespoon of soymilk
    2 tablespoons of maple syrup
    One fourth teaspoon of peppermint oil
    2 cups of Sucanat sugar flour

If mixture is too thick can add more soymilk one tablespoon at a time.

This can be used for cake or cookies

Apply when cake or cookies are cold

Notes: ────────────────────────

────────────────────────────

────────────────────────────

Recipe 414 _____

PINEAPPLE LEMON BAKED ALASKA

Place the following in a vitamix until smooth:

> One brick or 1 pound of tofu
> 1 cup of sucanant sugar
> 1 cup of maple syrup
> 1 cup of almond butter
> One fourth cup of lemon juice
> One fourth cup of pineapple juice

Place in six baking bowls 7 x 7 inches -- I use the same for pot pies.

Bake 350 degrees for 20 minutes

Let cool, Freeze extra

Notes: _____
_____
_____

Recipe 415

LEMON BAKED ALASKA

Place the following in a vitamix until smooth:

> One brick or 1 pound of tofu
> 1 cup of sucanant sugar
> 1 cup of maple syrup
> 1 cup of almond butter
> One fourth cup of lemon juice
> One fourth cup of lemon rind

Place in six baking bowls 7 x 7 inches -- I use the same for pot pies.

Bake 350 degrees for 20 minutes

Let cool Freeze extra

Notes: _____
_____
_____

Recipe 416 ────────────────

ORANGE BAKED ALASKA

Place the following in a vitamix until smooth:

> One brick or 1 pound of tofu
> 1 cup of sucanant sugar
> 1 cup of maple syrup
> 1 cup of almond butter
> One fourth cup of orange juice
> One fourth cup of orange rind

Place in six baking bowls 7 x 7 inches -- I use the same for potpies.

Bake 350 degrees for 20 minutes

Let cool, Freeze extra

Notes: _____
_____
_____

Recipe 417 —————————————————————————

PEPPERMINT BAKED ALASKA

Place the following in a vitamix until smooth:

  One brick or 1 pound of tofu
  1 cup of sucanant sugar
  1 cup of maple syrup
  1 cup of almond butter
  One fourth teaspoon of peppermint oil

Place in six baking bowls 7 x 7 inches -- I use the same for pot pies.

Bake 350 degrees for 20 minutes

Let cool serve cold Freeze extra

Notes: ————————————————————————————
————————————————————————————
————————————————————————————

Recipe 418

VANILLA BAKED ALASKA

Place the following in a vitamix until smooth:

    One brick or 1 pound of tofu
    1 cup of sucanant sugar
    1 cup of maple syrup
    1 cup of almond butter
    One tablespoon of vanilla

Place in six baking bowls 7 x 7 inches -- I use the same for potpies.

Bake 350 degrees for 20 minutes

Let cool, Freeze extra

Notes: _____

_____

_____

Recipe 419 _____

RED HOT FIRE SAUCE

Place the following in a vitamix

    2 cups of Havenaro peppers

    4 cups of crushed red peppers

    4 - 6 cups water

    2 tablespoons of garlic powder or four cloves of garlic

    1 cup of maple syrup

    One onion

    1 cup of cilantro

    1 cup of lemon juice

    2 tablespoons of Biosalt

    2 teaspoons of cumin

    26 -46 tomatoes

Boil for 2 hours on low (or until sauce is thick)

Notes: _____

_____

_____

Recipe 420

APRICOT ICE CREAM

Place in a vitamix the following:

    2 Cups of Maple syrup

    1 Tablespoon of Almond butter

    1 cup of Apricots (remove seeds only)

    2 cups of walnuts

    3 cups of Puffed Corn

    1 Brick or one pound of Tofu

    One fourth teaspoon of Biosalt

    One half cup of soymilk

    One cup of Pineapple juice or one more cup of soymilk

Mix until smooth

Pour into 6 ounce cups and freeze

Notes: _____

_____

_____

Recipe 421 _____

TWICE COOKED HERB POTATO

This recipe is for 4 - 6 potatoes approximately 6 inches long. The night before place 4 - 6 clean potatoes inside a brown paper bag and into the microwave oven for 7 - 8 minutes. To make sure inside is cooked stick a toothpick inside the center, if goes in easy it is cooked. Let cool - place in refrigerator. The next day place the following in a small pan and cook 5 - 10 minutes on low:

> One half teaspoon of Biosalt
> 1 tablespoon of Italian seasoning
> 1 cup of corn
> One half onion cut small
> One fourth cup of cilantro
> One half to one to one teaspoon garlic powder
> 3 tablespoons of lemon juice
> 3 tablespoons of Braggs

Mix and set aside

Cut each potato lengthwise and hollow out starting with the center with a spoon, leaving skin in tact.

Place the insides into a large bowl and add all of the above ingredients from the pan and mix.

Place back into potato shell and on a cookie sheet lined with cookie mat.

Bake 15 minutes at 350 degrees

Freeze extra

Notes: _____

_____

_____

Recipe 422

PEPPERMINT MACAROONS

Mix the following the night before and place in a refrigerator covered,

Place in a large bowl the following:

One fourth teaspoon of peppermint oil
6 cups of Maple syrup
4 cups of coconut
1 teaspoon of Biosalt
2 teaspoons of almond butter

Mix and add 5 cups of Whole Wheat Pastry flour sifted.

The next day place 2 spoons of the mixture, to form into a circle.

Place on trays lined with parchment paper or cookie mat.

Bake 325 degrees 25 minutes

Notes: _____

_____

_____

Recipe 423

PEACH ICE CREAM

Place in a vitamix the following:

    2 cups of maple syrup
    1 tablespoon of almond butter
    2 cups of walnuts
    1 cup of peaches (remove pits)
    3 cups of puffed rice
    one fourth teaspoon of Biosalt
    1 brick or 1 pound of tofu

Mix until all ingredients are smooth

Place into 6 ounce cups and freeze

Notes: _____

_____

_____

*Recipe 424*_____

TWICE COOKED SPICY RED POTATOES

This recipe is for 4 - 6 potatoes approximately 6 inches long. The night before place 4 - 6 clean potatoes inside a brown paper bad and into the microwave oven for 7 - 8 minutes. To make sure inside is cooked stick a toothpick inside the center, if goes in easy it is cooked. Let cool - place in refrigerator. The next day place the following in a small pan and cook 5 - 10 minutes on low:

One half teaspoon of Biosalt
1 cup of corn
1 shredded carrot
One half onion cut small
3 tablespoons of lemon juice
3 tablespoons of Braggs
1 teaspoon of chili powder
1 teaspoon of paprika
3 tablespoons of hot sauce

Mix and set aside

Cut each potato lengthwise and hollow out starting with the center with a spoon, leaving skin in tact.

Place the insides into a large bowl and add all of the above ingredients from the pan and mix.

Place back into potato shell and on a cookie sheet lined with cookie mat.

Bake 15 minutes at 350 degrees

Freeze extra

Notes: _____

_____

_____

Recipe 425

PLUM MACAROONS

Mix the following the night before and place in a refrigerator covered.

Place in a large bowl the following:

One cup of plums (fresh - remove pits only and cut into small parts)
6 cups of maple syrup
4 cups of coconut
1 teaspoon of Biosalt
2 teaspoons of almond butter

Mix and add 5 and a half cups to 6 cups of Whole wheat pastry flour sifted.

Dough will be thick.

The next day place 2 spoons of the mixture, to form into a circle.

Place on trays lined with parchment paper or cookie mat.

Bake 325 degrees 25 minutes

Notes: _____
_____
_____

Recipe 426

SPICY GARLIC SPREAD

Place into a large bowl the following:

  One third cup of cornmeal and another one third cup of cornmeal
  One half teaspoon of Biosalt
  2 cups of water

Mix and place into microwave oven for 5 minutes.

Place into vitamix the following:

  One and half teaspoons of Biosalt
  1 teaspoon of paprika
  1 cup of coconut
  1 teaspoon of chili powder
  3 and a half cups of water
  3 - 5 Habenaro peppers
  1 cup of sesame seeds
  1 cup of washed cashews
  8 tablespoons of lemon juice
  16 cloves of garlic

Mix and pour back into the large bowl and ad the following:

  2 tablespoons of onion flakes
  2 teaspoons of dill
  2 teaspoons of marjoram
  Spread on bread (recommend one loaf of Ezekiel Bread)

Place on trays lined with cookie mat.

Bake 350 degrees 10 minutes

can freeze extra

Notes:

Recipe 427

ITALIAN SPREAD

Place into a large bowl the following:

> One third cup of cornmeal and another one third cup of cornmeal.
> One half teaspoon of Biosalt
> 2 cups of water

Mix and place into microwave oven for 5 minutes.

Place into vitamix with the following:

> 2 tablespoons of Italian seasoning
> One and half teaspoons of Biosalt
> 1 cup of coconut
> 3 and a half cups of water
> 1 cup of sesame seeds
> 1 cup of washed cashews
> 8 tablespoons of lemon juice
> 16 cloves of garlic

Mix and pour back into the large bowl and add the following and mix.:

> 2 teaspoons of onion flakes
> 2 teaspoons of dill
> 2 teaspoons of marjoram
> Spread on bread (recommend one loaf of Ezekiel Bread)

Place on trays lined with cookie mat.

Bake 350 degrees 10 minutes

can freeze extra

Notes:

Recipe 428

WALNUT WAFFLES

Place the following in a Vitamix.

    6 cups of soymilk or water
    4 cups of Oatmeal
    1 cup of walnuts
    2 teaspoons of Biosalt
    One half cup of sesame seeds or almond butter

Mix and pour into waffle iron one spoon at a time spread evenly.

Cook 13 - 15 minutes. Let waffles cool and freeze extra.

When ready to rewarm place into toaster oven

Notes: _____

_____

_____

Recipe 429

POPPY SEED WAFFLES

Place the following in a Vitamix.

> One cup of poppy seeds
> 6 cups of soymilk or water
> 4 cups of Oatmeal
> 1 cup of walnuts
> 2 teaspoons of Biosalt
> One half cup of sesame seeds or almond butter

Mix and pour enough of mixture into waffle iron one spoon at a time spread evenly.

Cook 13 - 15 minutes. Let waffles cool and freeze extra.

When ready to rewarm place into toaster oven

Notes: _____

_____

_____

Recipe 430

PUMPKIN SEED WAFFLES

Place the following in a Vitamix.

> One cup of Pumpkin Seeds (unshelled)
> 6 cups of soymilk or water
> 4 cups of Oatmeal
> 1 cup of walnuts
> 2 teaspoons of Biosalt
> One half cup of sesame seeds or almond butter

Mix and pour enough of mixture into waffle iron one spoon at a time spread evenly.

Cook 13 - 15 minutes. Let waffles cool and freeze extra.

When ready to rewarm place into toaster oven

Notes: _____

_____

_____

Recipe 431 _____

CAROB SUCANANT SUGAR COOKIES

Place in a vitamix :

    2 teaspoons of Pineapple juice or water
    1 teaspoon of Biosalt
    3 cups of almond butter
    3 cups of maple syrup
    2 tablespoons of carob powder
    1 teaspoon of vanilla

Mix and pour into a large bowl and add:

    4 cups of whole wheat pastry flour sifted.

Mix and place this bowl covered in refrigerator. Do this the day before.

The next day rollout the dough -- instead of using flour on board pour sucanant sugar. Using a rolling pin make dough cookie thickness.

Can use any cookie cutter - shapes.

One to 2 pounds of sucanant sugar needed.

Place on trays lined with cookie mat.

Bake 10 - 13 minutes 375 degrees

Notes: _____

_____

_____

Recipe 432

ROMA SUCANANT SUGAR COOKIES

Place in a vitamix :

    2 teaspoons of Pineapple juice or water
    1 teaspoon of biosalt
    3 cups of almond butter
    3 cups of maple syrup
    2 teaspoons of Roma
    1 teaspoon of vanilla

Mix and pour into a large bowl and add:

    4 cups of whole wheat pastry flour sifted.

Mix and place this bowl covered in refrigerator. Do this the day before.

The next day rollout the dough -- instead of using flour on board pour sucanant sugar. Using a rolling pin make dough cookie thickness.

Can use any cookie cutter - shapes.

One to 2 pounds of sucanant sugar needed.

Place on trays lined with cookie mat.

Bake 10 - 13 minutes 375 degrees

Notes: _____

        _____

        _____

Recipe 433 _____

PEPPERMINT SUCANANT SUGAR COOKIES

Place in a vitamix:

    2 teaspoons of Pineapple juice or water
    1 teaspoon of Biosalt
    3 cups of almond butter
    3 cups of maple syrup
    One fourth to one half teaspoon of Peppermint oil
    1 teaspoon of vanilla

Mix and pour into a large bowl and add:

    4 cups of whole wheat pastry flour sifted.

Mix and place this bowl covered in refrigerator. Do this the day before.

The next day rollout the dough -- instead of using flour on board pour sucanant sugar. Using a rolling pin make dough cookie thickness.

Can use any cookie cutter - shapes.

One to 2 pounds of sucanant sugar needed.

Place on trays lined with cookie mat.

Bake 10 - 13 minutes 375 degrees

Notes: _____

_____

_____

Recipe 434

CINNAMON SUCANANT SUGAR COOKIES

Place in a vitamix :

    2 teaspoons of Pineapple juice or water
    1 teaspoon of Biosalt
    3 cups of almond butter
    3 cups of maple syrup
    2 tablespoons of Cinnamon
    1 teaspoon of vanilla

Mix and pour into a large bowl and add:

    4 cups of whole wheat pastry flour sifted.

Mix and place this bowl covered in refrigerator. Do this the day before.

The next day rollout the dough -- instead of using flour on board pour sucanant sugar. Using a rolling pin make dough cookie thickness.

Can use any cookie cutter - shapes.

One to 2 pounds of sucanant sugar needed.

Place on trays lined with cookie mat.

Bake 10 - 13 minutes 375 degrees

Notes: _____

_____

_____

Recipe 435

GINGER SUCANANT SUGAR COOKIES

Place in a vitamix :

> 2 teaspoons of Pineapple juice or water
> 1 teaspoon of Biosalt
> 3 cups of almond butter
> 3 cups of maple syrup
> 1 to 2 teaspoons of Ginger
> 1 teaspoon of vanilla

Mix and pour into a large bowl and add:

> 4 cups of whole wheat pastry flour sifted.

Mix and place this bowl covered in refrigerator. Do this the day before.

The next day rollout the dough -- instead of using flour on board pour sucanant sugar. Using a rolling pin make dough cookie thickness.

Can use any cookie cutter - shapes.

One to 2 pounds of sucanant sugar needed.

Place on trays lined with cookie mat.

Bake 10 - 13 minutes 375 degrees

Notes: _____

_____

_____

*Recipe 436*_____

CAROB SUGARED NUTS

Mix in a large bowl the following:

One cup of each:

Walnuts
Pecans
Almonds
Hazel Nuts
Brazil Nuts
Maple Syrup

Can substitute if one nut is not available. Example 2 cups of walnuts instead of hazel nuts.

Mix and add:

1 teaspoon of Biosalt
2 tablespoons of carob powder
2 cups of sucanant sugar

Mix and pour on cookie sheet lined with cookie mat.

Bake 200 degrees for 12 hours or more.

One tray in oven only.

Let cool and store in refrigerator

Notes: _____
_____
_____

Recipe 437

ROMA SUGARED NUTS

Mix in a large bowl the following:

One cup of each:

> Walnuts
> Pecans
> Almonds
> Hazel Nuts
> Brazil Nuts
> Maple Syrup

Can substitute if one nut is not available. Example 2 cups of walnuts instead of hazel nuts.

Mix and add:

> 1 teaspoon of Biosalt
> 2 tablespoons Roma
> 2 cups of sucanant sugar

Mix and pour on cookie sheet lined with cookie mat.

Bake 200 degrees for 12 hours or more.

One tray in oven only.

Let cool and store in refrigerator

Notes: _____
_____
_____

Recipe 438

PECAN PIE

See special pie crust recipe # 38

In a bowl mix the following:

    1 cup of sucanant sugar
    One half cup of almond butter
    1 teaspoon of vanilla
    One half cup of tofu

Mix and add 2 cups of chopped pecans.

Mix and add to uncooked pie crust. When all ingredients are in shell level with back of spoon and pour 1 cup of maples syrup on top of the pie.

Bake 375 degrees for 25 minutes.

Notes: _____

_____

_____

Recipe 439

BLUEBERRY CREAM PIE

See special pie crust recipe #38

Place in a vitamix the following:

One and half pounds of Blueberries (do not add any water)

and add the following:

1 cup of maple syrup
1 cup of sucanant sugar
2 large apples or 4 small apples (remove the cores)
One fourth teaspoon of Biosalt

Pour mixture into large pan and boil for 1 hour or more on warm until thick.

Pour mixture into pie shell. Place top crust. (See piecrust recipe #38 cut recipe in half or else will be too much crust) Do not add any maple syrup.

This is a crumb crust. Cover pie and press into pie.

Bake 350 degrees 45 minutes

Let Cool and cut. Freeze extra

Notes: _____

_____

_____

Recipe 440

GRAPE CREAM PIE

See special pie crust recipe # 38

Place in a vitamix the following:

    3 cups of grapes (can use any seedless variety)

and add the following:

    1 cup of maple syrup
    1 cup of sucanant sugar
    2 large apples or 4 small apples (remove the cores)
    One fourth teaspoon of Biosalt

Pour mixture into large pan and boil for 1 hour or more on warm until thick.

Pour mixture into pie shell. Place top crust. (See pie crust recipe # 38 cut recipe in half or else will be too much crust) Do not add any maple syrup.

This is a crumb crust. Cover pie and press into pie.

Bake 350 degrees 45 minutes

Let Cool and cut. Freeze extra

Notes: _____

_____

_____

Recipe 441 _____

LEMON FROSTING

Place in a vitamix the following:

    6 cup of sucanant sugar (3 cups at a time)

make into a fine powder.

Pour into a bowl and add:

    3 tablespoons of maple syrup

Mix and add

    6 tablespoons of Lemon Juice (one tablespoon at a time)

this will make mixture thinner.

Place on cake only when cold.

Place back into refrigerator uncovered.

Serve cold

Notes: _____

_____

_____

Recipe 442

ORANGE CAKE FROSTING

Place in a vitamix the following:

    6 cup of sucanant sugar (3 cups at a time)

make into a fine powder.

Pour into a bowl and add:

    3 tablespoons of maple syrup

Mix and add

    6 tablespoons of Orange Juice (one tablespoon at a time)

This will make mixture thinner.

Place on cake only when cold.

Place back into refrigerator uncovered.

Serve cold

Notes: _____

_____

_____

Recipe List

1. BAKED POTATO
2. SALADS
3. PASTA
4. PASTA SAUCE - TOMATO SAUCE
5. BROWN RICE
6. TEXAN RICE
7. BELL PEPPER RICE
8. TOSTADAS
9. POPCORN
10. HOT SAUCE
11. CINDY HUCK BEANS FOR BURRITOS
12. TODD NEUMILLER CHINESE SOUP
13. ALMOND BUTTER
14. PIZZA SAUCE
15. PIZZA DOUGH (FOR PIES)
16. WAFFLES
17. TAMALE CASSEROLE
18. MAPLE SYRUP CAKE
19. PAN - FRIED NOODLES
20. FRUIT ICING
21. CAROB BAKED ALASKA
22. VANILLA CAKE
23. CAROB GLAZE
24. MAPLE OATMEAL CAKE
25. CLOVE COOKIES
26. DONALD W. HUCK COCONUT COOKIES

27. CAROB ROMA OATMEAL COOKIES

28. DEEP - DISH PIZZA

29. COCONUT OATMEAL CAROB ROMA COOKIES

30. COCONUT OATMEAL COOKIES

31. CAROB ROMA COCONUT OATMEAL WHOLE-WHEAT PASTRY FLOUR COOKIES

32. COCONUT OATMEAL WHOLE WHEAT PASTRY FLOUR COOKIES

33. STUFFED BELL PAPPERS

34. MAPLE SYRUP COOKIES

35. CAROB COOKIES

36. CAROB BROWN CAKE

37. ANY FRUIT COOKIES (PEACH, CHERRY, APRICOT)

38. SPECIAL PIE CRUST

39. PUMPKIN PIE

40. PARVIN MALEK CAROB PIE

41. ALMOND BUTTER COOKIES 2

42. CAROB FILLING

43. EVELYN ANN MENZIE OLD-FASHIONED GLAZE

44. PINEAPPLE PIE

45. BUTTER COOKIES

46. SUCANANT COOKIES

47. INEZ A. MENZIE COCONUT COOKIES

48. TURNOVERS

49. GOLDEN MACAROONS

50. ORIENTAL CRUNCH

51. PINEAPPLE CANDY

52. CAROB DOUGHNUTS

53. LEMON DOUGHNUTS

54. GRAIN PIZZA

55. CORNMEAL PIZZA

56. CAROB BROWNIES

57. ROBERT E MENZIE WALNUT PIE

58. APRICOT COCONUT WALNUT SQUARES

59. PISTACHIO SCONES

60. EGG ROLLS

61. ROASTED SALTED NUTS

62. FUDGE CUP COOKIE

63. FUDGE SAUCE

64. PINEAPPLE COOKIES

65. TAMALE BEAN PIE

66. NUT PIE

67. DATE WALNUT COOKIES

68. CARAMELIZED GINGER HAZELNUT TART

69. PAPAYA COOKIES

70. CAJUN MIXED NUTS

71. TACO SALAD SHELLS

72. FOR CAKE-WEDDING STYLE CAKE

73. SPANISH MILLET CASSEROLE

74. ENCHILADAS

75. CAROB PIE

76. NUT BUTTER BALLS

77. SHARAREH SHABAFROOZ GARLIC BREAD SPREAD/BUTTER

78. GLAZED CARROT CAKE

79. WAFFLES WITH CASHEWS AND OATMEAL

80. LEMON PINEAPPLE PIE

81. CORN BREAD

82. MATTHEW F. MOONEY ROAST FOR ANY HOLIDAY

83. SPICE DOUGHNUTS

84. SPANISH RICE

85. PINEAPPLE SANDWICH COOKIE

86. CAROB CUP COOKIE

87. ANY FRUIT CUP COOKIE

88. SETAREH TAIS CAKE

89. CAROB DATE PISTACHIO PASTRY

90. FRUIT CAKE COOKIE

91. BAKED MILLET

92. BISCOTTI

93. MULTIGRAIN CRACKERS

94. POT PIE

95. BASIC COOKIE WITH FROSTING

96. TACO SHELLS

97. ANY FRUIT PASTRY

98. PINEAPPLE FROSTING

99. PINEAPPLE UPSIDE DOWN CAKE

100. HOT BEANS FOR BURRITOS

101. APRICOT PIE

102. APPLE PIE

103. PLUM PIE

104. PIZZA SAUCE NO. 3

105. PIZZA SAUCE NO. 1

106. COFFEE MUFFINS

107. GLORIA DUGGINS PECAN CANDY

108. PETER P. PANAGOPOULOS ALMOND FUDGE

109. PETE/ROSA CERRILLO CINNAMON WALNUT CANDY

110. SUGARED NUTS

111. PAPAYA CANDY

112. CAROB CAKE

113. THELMA MAIN HAZELNUT FUDGE

114. WHEAT CORNMEAL PIZZA

115. MARGARET/HARVEY BINDER PECAN FUDGE

116. MICHAEL F. MOONEY PECAN ROMA CAROB CANDY

117. BELLE HUCK WALNUT FUDGE

118. SAUCE FOR INSIDE CINNAMON ROLLS

119. NECTARINE PIE

120. COOKIES/CAROB PLAIN OR ROMA

121. CAROB BARS

122. SPICE BUTTER COOKIES

123. OAT CRACKERS

124. CINNAMON SUGAR DOUGHNUT TOPPING

125. JELLY DOUGHNUT FILLING

126. STRUDEL DOUGH

127. DATE CUP COOKIE

128. ITALIAN SAUCE

129. LASAGNA

130. BOB PANAGOPOULOS PIZZA SAUCE NO. 2

131. CUBAN BLACK BEANS IN RICE

132. BLACK BEANS

133. LIGHT FUDGE

134. DARK FUDGE

135. PIGEON BEANS

136. XENIA PANAGOPOULOS PIGEON RICE

137. ALEXANDRA PANAGOPOULOS SWEET AND SOUR SAUCE NO. 1

138. INEZ SPEIDELL SWEET AND SOUR SAUCE NO. 2

139. VERY VERY HOT SAUCE

140. LENTILS

141. SHRIMP SAUCE

142. GABRIEL CERRILLO ALMOND CAROB CANDY

143. CAROB ROMA CANDY

144. WALNUT CINNAMON CLUSTERS

145. TAMARA NEUMILLER SPANISH PASTA

146. CHINESE RICE

147. CHILI BEANS

148. TAMALES

149. VEGETABLE SOUP

150. CAROB ROMA COOKIES

151. RAY AND LINDA PANAGOPOULOS SUNFLOWER COCONUT WAFFLES

152. WAFFLES OATMEAL AND ALMONDS

153. RHI CAROB AND ROMA OATMEAL WWP NUTLESS COOKIE

154. HOT SAUCE

155. RED BEANS FOR TOP OF RICE

156. CORN MEAL WAFFLES

157. TAGLIATELLE SAUCE

158. ALMOND BUTTER COOKIES

159. MAPLE SYRUP FROSTING

160. ORANGE GLAZE

161. RYE PANCAKES

162. PANCAKES

163. BLUEBERRY TOPPING

164. ROMA ICE CREAM

165. LEMON ICE CREAM

166. ORANGE DATE SYRUP

167. CAROB FUDGE SAUCE

168. COCONUT LIME FROSTING

169. CREAMY FROSTING

198. PUMPKIN COOKIES

199. MARSELLAS PANAGOPOULOS BRAZIL NUT ICE CREAM

200. TAHEREH MALEK PUMPKIN ICE CREAM

201. BAKED BROWN RICE

202. GINGER CANDY

203. SANDY MOONEY COFFEE CAKE

204. PAPAYA WALNUT COOKIES

205. LEMON CARROT COOKIES

206. CAROB SANDWICH COOKIES

207. DAISY FROSTING

208. BLACK-EYED PEAS

209. ALMOND BUTTER FROSTING

210. CRUNCH TOPPING FOR ANY BAKED PIE

211. CHERI GILBERT COOKED CAROB GLAZE

212. SUCANANT SUGAR GLAZE

213. ROMA CREAM FROSTING

214. LEMON FILLING

215. BAR-B-QUE SAUCE

216. TOFU FROSTING

217. SWEET SUGAR ICING

218. BLACK EYED IN RICE

219. SOY MILK CORNBREAD

220. OATMEAL ALMOND COOKIE

221. SPICED CUPCAKES

222. DATE OATMEAL COOKIE

223. ORANGE COCONUT COOKIE

224. DATE COOKIE BAR

225. APRICOT COOKIE BAR

226. GINGER PANCAKES

227. LEMON PASTRY

228. LEMON SUGAR COOKIES

229. DATE BROWNIES

230. ORIGINAL SALT WATER TAFFY

231. AURA VICTORIA HUCK PEPPERMINT SALT WATER TAFFY

232. LEMON SALT WATER TAFFY

233. VANILLA SALT WATER TAFFY

234. ORANGE SALT WATER TAFFY

235. JACK PANAGOPOULOS ROMA SALT WATER TAFFY

236. ADRIANA CERRILLO PECAN SALT WATER TAFFY

237. ELMER LYLE MENZIE ALMOND SALT WATER TAFFY

238. ASHLEY SPEIDELL WALNUT SALT WATER TAFFY

239. ROSS H. MENZIE CAROB SALT WATER TAFFY

240. COCONUT SALT WATER TAFFY

241. CINAMMON SALT WATER TAFFY

242. GINGER SALT WATER TAFFY

243. GENE KOENIG ENGLISH TOFFEE CANDY

244. LUCILLE GILBERT LEMON CHEESECAKE

245. ORANGE CHEESECAKE

246. ASHER MICHAEL NEUMILLER CAROB CHEESECAKE

247. ALLIE NICOLE BLUMA NEUMILLER CAROB CAKE

248. DR. EDE VANILLA SUGAR CAKE

249. WALNUT SQUARE COOKIES

250. TARA SHABAFROOZ PECAN SQUARE COOKIES

251. ALMOND SQUARE COOKIES

252. MARGRET ANN MENZIE PECAN ROPE COOKIES

253. MASSOOD SHABAFROOZ WALNUT ROPE COOKIES

254. ALMOND ROPE COOKIES

255. RHI COCONUT OATMEAL CAROB AND ROMA COOKIES

256. RHI COCONUT OATMEAL COOKIES

257. RHI COCONUT OATMEAL WHOLE WHEAT PASTRY FLOUR COOKIES

258. RHI CAROB COCONUT COOKIES

259. RHI COCONUT COOKIES

260. RHI CAROB AND ROMA OATMEAL COOKIES

261. RHI VANILLA DONUTS OR CAKE

262. RHI CAROB BROWN CAKE

263. RHI GOLDEN MACAROONS

264. RHI COFFEE MUFFINS

265. RHI SPICED CUP CAKES

266. PEPPERMINT WALNUT FUDGE

267. PEPPERMINT ICE CREAM

268. CAROB AND ROMA ICE CREAM

269. CHERRY FUDGE

270. CAROB ROMA PEPPERMINT ICE CREAM

271. PEACH APRICOT PIE

272. ROMA BAKED ALASKA

273. RAISIN BAR COOKIES

274. FREDERICK HUCK POCKET BREAD FOLDING DIAGRAM

275. NOOSHIN MALEK SEE MOUSEH

276. ZOHREH EHSANI BLUEBERRY ICE CREAM

277. POCKET PIZZA 1

278. RAISIN CREAM PIE

279. DR. EDE KOENIG BEEROCK

280. DATE CREAM PIE

281. POCKET RAISIN PASTRY

282. POCKET PIZZA 3

283. POCKET PIZZA 4

284. POCKET PIZZA 2

285. POCKET DATE PASTRY

286. POCKET PLUM PASTRY

287. PLUM CREAM PIE

288. POCKET CAROB PASTRY

289. POCKET ROMA PASTRY

290. POCKET WALNUT PASTRY

291. POCKET APRICOT PASTRY

292. POCKET CHERRY PASTRY

293. POCKET PEACH PASTRY

294. POCKET PINEAPPLE - LEMON PASTRY

295. POCKET PUMPKIN PASTRY

296. POCKET APPLE PASTRY

297. POCKET EGG ROLLS

298. POCKET BEAN BURRITO

299. APRICOT CREAM PIE

300. VERA WALDSCHMIDT CHERRY CREAM PIE

301. PEACH CREAM PIE

302. APPLE CREAM PIE

303. TAHEREH TAHERIAN HAVANERO HOT SAUCE

304. SHAHNAZ SHAINEE HOT AND SPICY PINTO BEANS

305. PAYAM MALEK ZADEH CAROB WHEAT COOKIES

306. RAISIN ICE CREAM

307. TOMATO CASSEROLE

308. RAISIN FACE COOKIE

309. DATE FACE COOKIE

310. PINEAPPLE COCONUT SQUARES

311. ORANGE PINEAPPLE ICE CREAM

312. LEMON PINEAPPLE ICE CREAM

313. ROMA FACE COOKIE

314. CAROB FACE COOKIE

315. PUMPKIN FACE COOKIE

316. PINEAPPLE FACE COOKIE

317. APPLE FACE COOKIE

318. PEACH FACE COOKIE

319. APRICOT FACE COOKIE

320. PLUM FACE COOKIE

321. CHERRY FACE COOKIE

322. WALNUT DOME COOKIES

323. ALMOND DOME COOKIES

324. PECAN DOME COOKIES

325. CAROB DOME COOKIES

326. ROMA DOME COOKIES

327. COFFEE CUP COOKIE

328. RAISIN CUP COOKIE

329. WALNUT CUP COOKIE

330. POCKET PASTA NO. 4

331. POCKET PASTA NO. 2

332. POCKET PASTA NO. 3

333. POCKET PASTA NO. 1

334. BRAZIL NUT CARMEL CANDY

335. HAVANERO BAKED RICE

336. MACADAMA CARMEL CANDY

337. CINNAMON CARMEL CANDY

338. WALNUT CARMEL CANDY

339. COCONUT CARMEL CANDY

340. PECAN CARMEL CANDY

341. PISTACHIO CARMEL CANDY

342. HAZEL NUT CARMEL CANDY

343. CASHEW CARMEL CANDY

344. ROASTED ALMOND CARMEL CANDY

345. LEMON CARMEL CANDY

346. ORANGE CARMEL CANDY

347. CAROB CARMEL CANDY

348. ROMA CARMEL CANDY

349. PEPPERMINT CARMEL CANDY

350. GINGER CARMEL CANDY

351. HERBS & GARLIC BAKED RICE

352. WALNUT & ALMOND FROSTING

353. PINEAPPLE & LEMON GLAZE

354. ROMA TOFU COOKIES

355. CAROB TOFU COOKIES

356. CINNAMON TOFU COOKIES

357. RAISIN TOFU COOKIES

358. APRICOT TOFU COOKIES

359. DATE TOFU COOKIES

360. CRANBERRIE TOFU COOKIES

361. SPICE TOFU COOKIES

362. PAPAYA TOFU COOKIES

363. COCONUT TOFU COOKIES

364. LEMON TOFU COOKIES

365. ORANGE TOFU COOKIES

366. PINEAPPLE TOFU COOKIES

367. BLACK BEAN SOUP

368. LEMON COCONUT COOKIES

369. CHERRY SUGAR COOKIES

370. ORANGE SUGAR COOKIES

371. RAISIN SUGAR COOKIES

372. ROMA SUGAR COOKIES

373. APPLE SUGAR COOKIES

374. CAROB SUGAR COOKIES

375. PEPPERMINT SUGAR COOKIES

376. BLUEBERRY SUGAR COOKIE

377. DATE SUGAR COOKIE

378. PINEAPPLE SUGAR COOKIE

379. PLUM SUGAR COOKIE

380. PEACH SUGAR COOKIE

381. APRICOT SUGAR COOKIE

382. NECTURINE SUGAR COOKIE

383. CRANBERRY SUGAR COOKIE

384. PUMPKIN SUGAR COOKIE

385. COCONUT CAROB CARMEL CANDY

386. COCONUT LEMON CARMEL CANDY

387. COCONUT CINNAMON CARMEL CANDY

388. COCONUT ORANGE CARMEL CANDY

389. COCONUT PEPPERMINT CARMEL CANDY

390. COCONUT PERO CARMEL CANDY

391. COCONUT GINGER CARMEL CANY

392. DATE OATMEAL COOKIE

393. RAISIN OATMEAL COOKIE

394. WALNUT DATE COOKIE

395. WALNUT LEMON COOKIE

396. WALNUT RAISIN COOKIE

397. WALNUT ORANGE COOKIE

398. WALNUT CHERRY COOKIE

399. COCONUT DATE COOKIE

400. COCONUT CHERRY COOKIE

401. COCONUT RAISIN COOKIE

402. ONION DRIED ROASTED NUTS

403. GARLIC DRIED ROASTED NUTS

404. HAVANERO DRIED ROASTED NUTS

405. CAYANE DRIED ROASTED NUTS

406. BLACK BEAN RICE

407. SALTED-HABANERO DRIED ROASTED NUT MIX

408. MAPLE SYRUP DRIED ROASTED NUTS

409. CAROB MACAROONS

410. LEMON MACAROONS

411. ROMA MACAROONS

412. ORANGE MACAROONS

413. PEPPERMINT FROSTING

414. PINEAPPLE-LEMON BAKED ALASKA

415. LEMON BAKED ALASKA

416. ORANGE BAKED ALASKA

417. PEPERMINT BAKED ALASKA

418. VANILLA BAKED ALASKA

419. RED HOT FIRE SAUCE

420. APRICOT ICE CREAM

421. TWICE COOKED HERB POTATO

422. PEPPERMINT MACROONS

423. PEACH ICE CREAM

424. TWICE COOKED SPICY POTATO

425. PLUM MACROONS

426. SPICY GARLIC SPREAD

427. ITALIAN SPREAD

428. WALNUT WAFFLES

429. POPPY SEED WAFFLES

430. PUMPKIN SEED WAFFLES

431. CAROB SUCANAT SUGAR COOKIE

432. ROMA SUCANAT SUGAR COOKIE

433. PEPPERMINT SUCANAT SUGAR COOKIE

434. CINNAMON SUCANAT SUGAR COOKIE

435. GINGER SUCANAT SUGAR COOKIE

436. CAROB SUGARED NUTS

437. ROMA SUGARED NUTS

438. PECAN PIE

439. BLUEBERRY CREAM PIE

440. GRAPE PIE

441. LEMON FROSTING

442. ORANGE CAKE FROSTING

Ingredients To Avoid

Bha-butylated bht hydroytolune

Black Strap Molasses

Caffeine

Calcium Sulfate

Carmel

Carrageen

Disodium Sulfite

Distilled water - (do not use- no minerals)

Edtacalcium disodium

Ethylenediamine

Letracetate

Gum Arabic

Cellulose chatti karaya

Gypsum

Hydroylated lecithin

Monocalcium Satisfactory Phosphate

Hydrolyzed protein

Lactic Acid

Magnesium chlorate

Maltodextrim - white sugar

Magnesium Sterate

Modified food starch

Mono+dislycerides

Mono sodium glutamate

M S G

Multol dextrin

Natural flavor

Nisarl

Non hydroxylated Lecithin

Phosforic acid

Popylgallate

Propylene Glycolalginate

Polysorbate 60, 65, 80
Red Dye 40 - Allura Red AC
Stearic Acid
Sodium Saccharin
Sodium Alginate
Sodium Benzoate
Sodium Bicarbonate
Sodium Chloride
Sodium Erythrobate
Sulfur Dioxide
Sugar black paperbicarbonate of soda
Tragacanth Xanthan
Torutein
Vinegar
Yeast flakes

References

Dr Ede Koenig

Hans Diehl Dr. H S C
(To your health)

J. Shirley Sweeney, MD

James W. Anderson, MD

About the Author

Diabetes no longer exists in my life. To date I have been diabetes free for almost ten years. I look at diabetes as unnecessary, unwanted, and a very poor choice to live with and maintain. My hope is that the readers of my books can say the same. The methods contained in this book are very doable. And much easier than most people initially believe. As a past diabetic, I have found that eating the right foods has been easy. Not having to live with diabetes is just another problem solved for me and a higher quality of life has been achieved.

Eating food with nutrition, maintaining a clean colon, and doing some exercise has been a very good trade instead of being a diabetic with all the problems. I have developed over six hundred delicious recipes and believe that there is absolutely no reason to eat junk food, which is the primary true cause of diabetes. The secondary cause of diabetes is a dirty colon, which causes the body's P. H. (potential hydrogen) to be off enough to malfunction which is called diabetes. Being a diabetic is no way to live. Your body is naturally warning you to stop eating junk food or fake foods. Just taking drugs and wasting your time in the doctors office and not eliminating the cause of diabetes, equals the maintaining of diabetes for life. A major side effect not widely known to a diabetic is the lack of circulation throughout the body. This side effect is caused mainly by the free oils that are found in animal products. This produces thicker blood, where the cells are sticking together which means less oxygen is traveling throughout the body. This lack of oxygen is the number one reason of amputation, for also some people a loss of limbs, toes, feet and or legs. There are other negative facts of being a diabetic. I urge everyone to take control of their food intake as I did.

The reader will see and feel his body is healing itself and the body will again function the way it was designed to work and you will regain your radiant health. I am so excited about my discoveries of good health through good food that I have made extra time to share my food, enter cooking contests, and develop more food recipes and share my findings so that others may have the same great health that I now have.